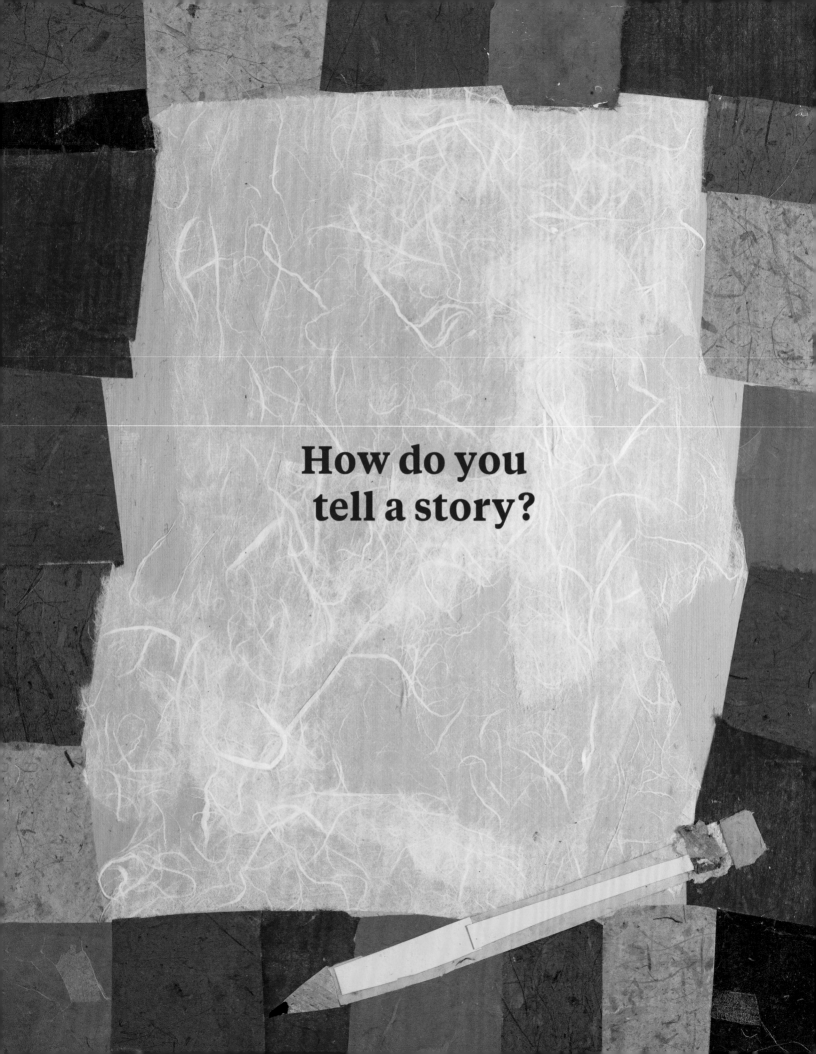

How do you
tell a story?

First, remember: your parents moved North with thousands more in the Great Migration, fleeing cruelty and unfairness down South and chasing dreams of a *big city life*.

You, Chloe Ardelia Wofford,
must listen before you tell your first tale.
Listen to your mother singing as she hangs
laundry and washes dishes.

Her voice is the *most beautiful ever.*
Hear the lore passed back and forth
between young and old in your family.

Listen to your mother's ghost stories
and your grandfather's violin.
Fiddling that gets the whole family on their feet.

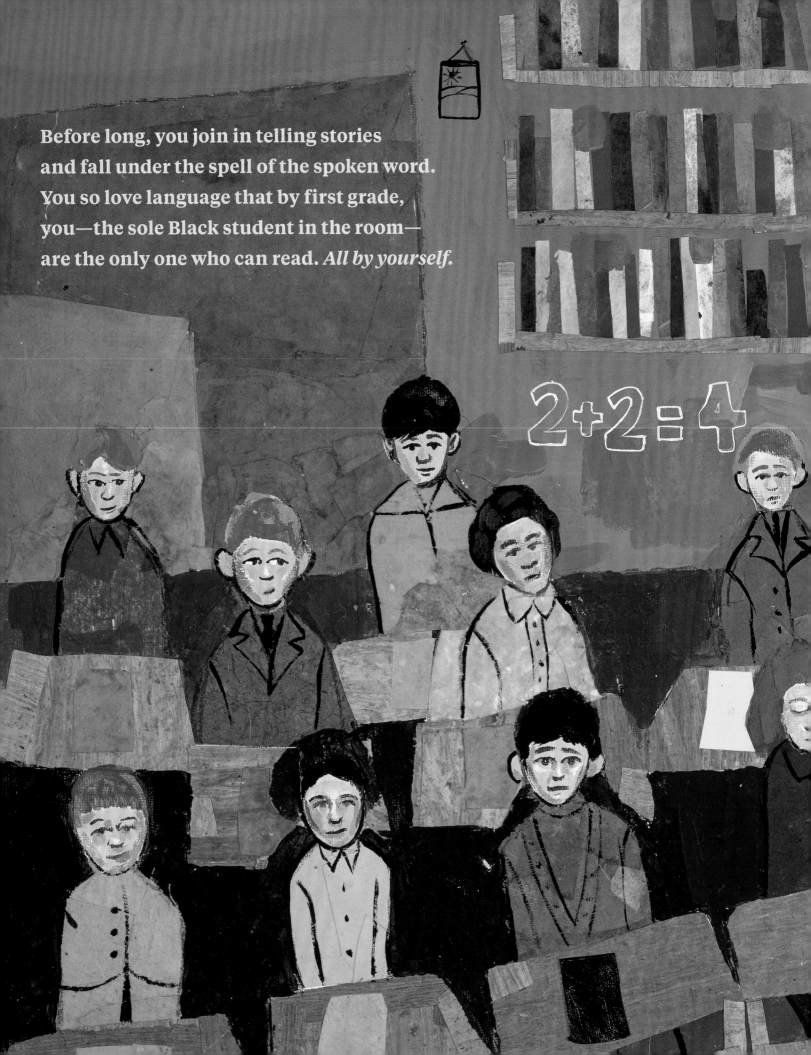

Before long, you join in telling stories
and fall under the spell of the spoken word.
You so love language that by first grade,
you—the sole Black student in the room—
are the only one who can read. *All by yourself.*

2+2=4

No one can call you second-class.
That means a lot at a time when laws and leaders
keep Blacks at the bottom of the ladder.
Your family may not have much money,
but your mother joins the Book of the Month Club.
In the Wofford household, books are everywhere.
You devour them like Sunday supper.

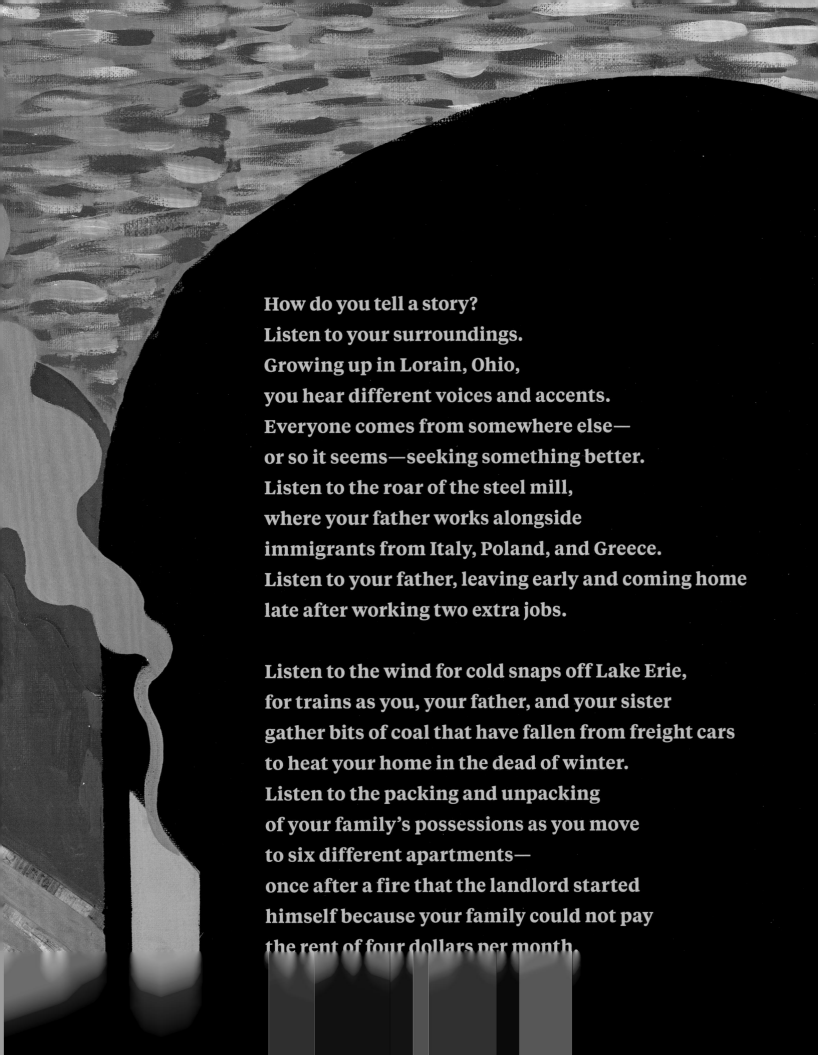

How do you tell a story?
Listen to your surroundings.
Growing up in Lorain, Ohio,
you hear different voices and accents.
Everyone comes from somewhere else—
or so it seems—seeking something better.
Listen to the roar of the steel mill,
where your father works alongside
immigrants from Italy, Poland, and Greece.
Listen to your father, leaving early and coming home
late after working two extra jobs.

Listen to the wind for cold snaps off Lake Erie,
for trains as you, your father, and your sister
gather bits of coal that have fallen from freight cars
to heat your home in the dead of winter.
Listen to the packing and unpacking
of your family's possessions as you move
to six different apartments—
once after a fire that the landlord started
himself because your family could not pay
the rent of four dollars per month.

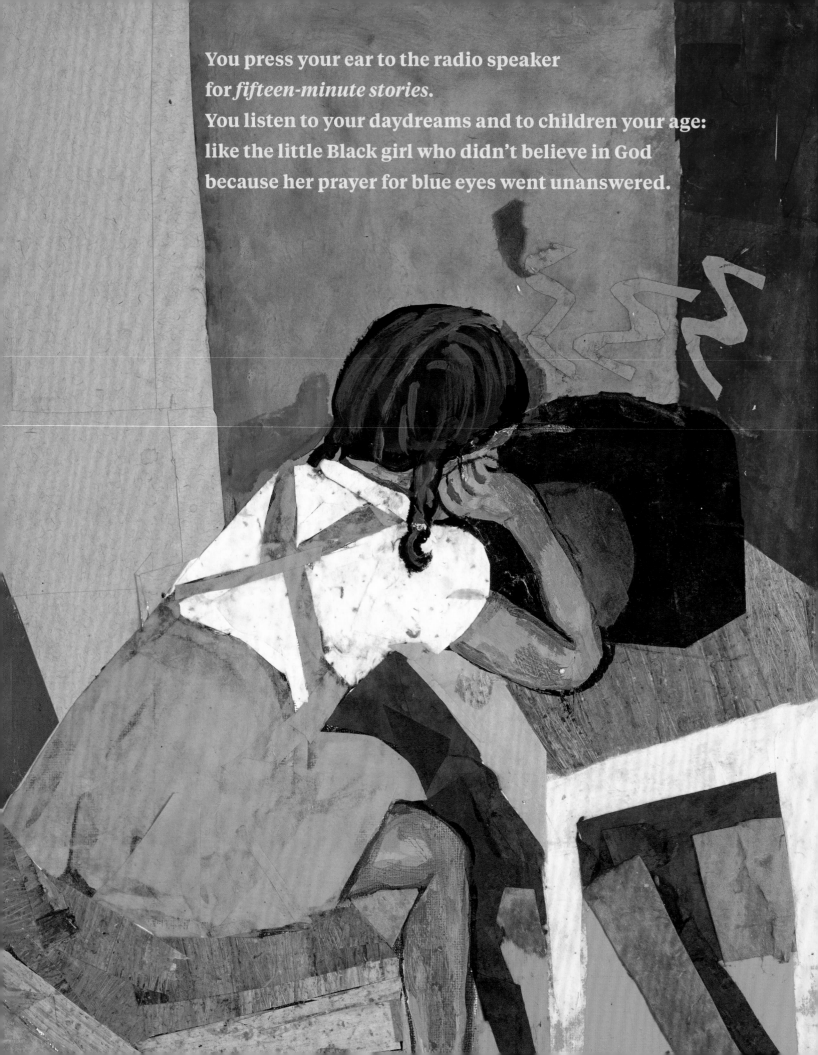

You press your ear to the radio speaker
for *fifteen-minute stories*.
You listen to your daydreams and to children your age:
like the little Black girl who didn't believe in God
because her prayer for blue eyes went unanswered.

QUIET, PLEASE

You listen as the priest leads Latin mass
and gives you your baptismal name—
Anthony—after the saint.
On the school debate team
and in the drama club, you find your own voice.
Your sister gets you a part-time job at the library.
Amid the stacks, you are in heaven.
You learn to listen to your own mind
telling you what to explore, *what to create.*

You hear pride in your parents' goodbyes
when you go off to college; the first in your family
to do so. At Howard University in Washington, DC,
another student mistakenly calls you Toni.
You chuckle and then take the name—
reminding you of your patron saint.
You're tired of hearing your name
mispronounced anyhow: Chlo, Chlorey, or Chlovee.
From now on, you are Toni.

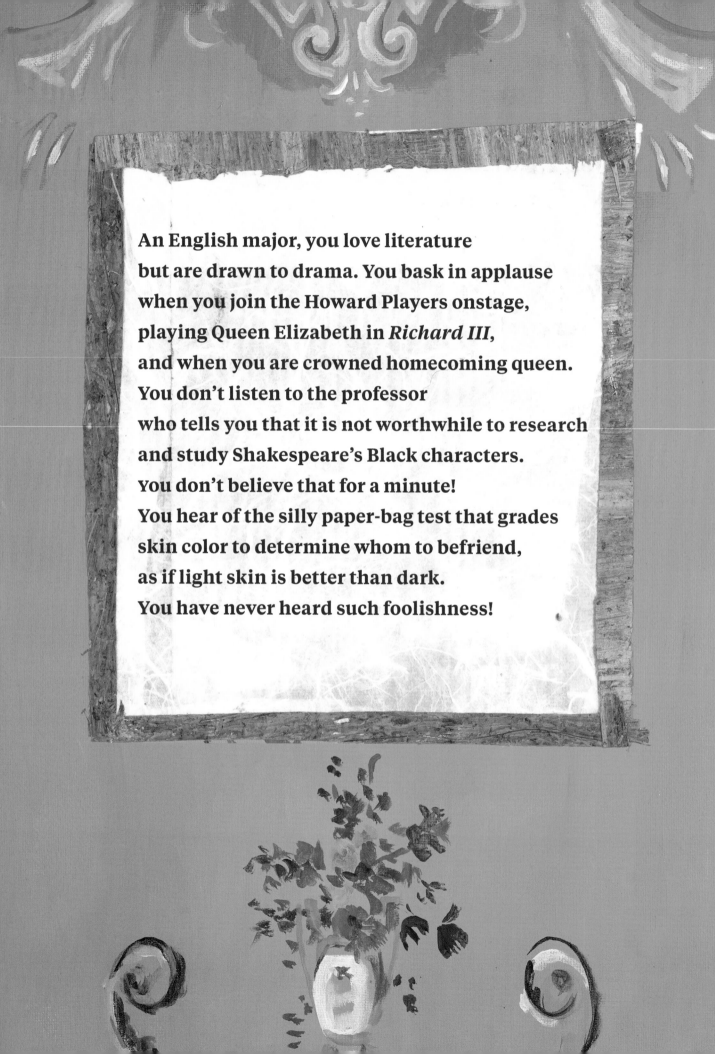

An English major, you love literature
but are drawn to drama. You bask in applause
when you join the Howard Players onstage,
playing Queen Elizabeth in *Richard III*,
and when you are crowned homecoming queen.
You don't listen to the professor
who tells you that it is not worthwhile to research
and study Shakespeare's Black characters.
You don't believe that for a minute!
You hear of the silly paper-bag test that grades
skin color to determine whom to befriend,
as if light skin is better than dark.
You have never heard such foolishness!

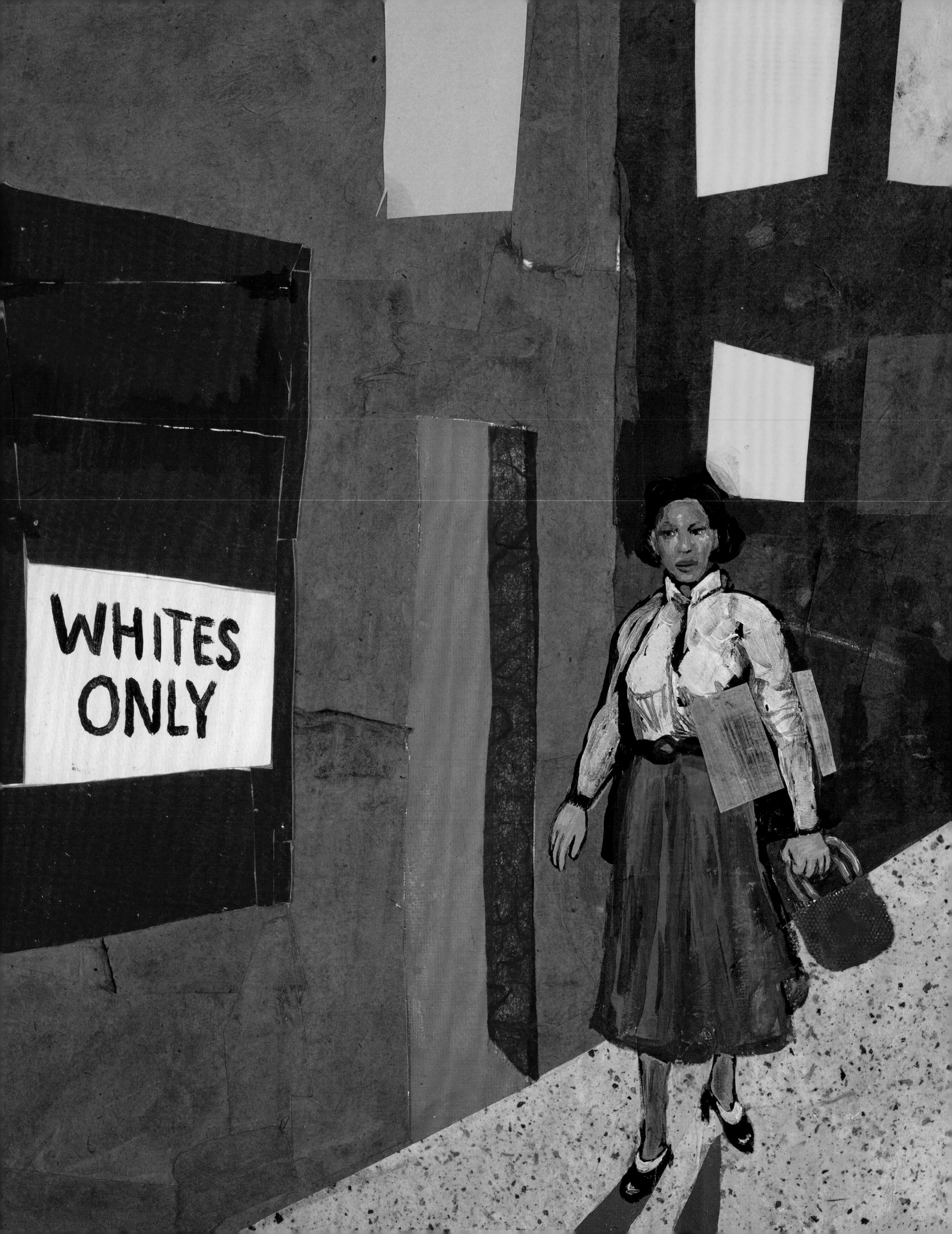
WHITES
ONLY

Downtown in the nation's capital,
you see Whites-Only signs for the first time.
You steal one from a city bus and send it home
to your mother to show her that racism
still raises its head in the capital of democracy.
When mail comes from home,
you listen for coins and cans of tuna and sardines
inside care packages your mother sends from the tips
she earns working in an amusement park's restroom.

Later, you listen to the footsteps of marchers
and the rallying cry of Dr. King,
a drum major for justice if there ever was one.
You heed the call to conscience in your own way,
vowing to write about and *for* Black people.
In the freedom struggle, *a pen will be your sword.*

When you yourself become a professor,
you listen to students at the Black colleges
where you teach English, and to the members
of the writers group, whose feedback
helps you to shape your works in progress.

You listen to your heart, marry a fellow professor, and start a family. And when that brief marriage ends, you listen to your head and move to Syracuse, New York, taking an editorial job to support your two sons.

You rise to senior editor—the first Black person
to hold that job in the entire publishing business.
With the power of words in your hands,
you listen to your inner voice, and perhaps
to ancestral spirits that were there all along.
When Blacks are overlooked and underrepresented,
you champion their genius
and usher Black lyrics and stories into print:
the jazz poetry of Henry Dumas,
the autobiography of boxer Muhammad Ali,
the powerful and revolutionary ideas
of activists Angela Davis and Huey P. Newton,
and the brilliant novels
of Toni Cade Bambara and Gayl Jones.
As an editor, *you let their lights shine*.

THEY CAME BEFORE COLUMBUS

CREOLE FEAST

WOMEN, RACE & CLASS

PLAY EBONY PLAY IVORY

BLOOD IN MY EYE

ROPE OF WIND

the sea birds are still alive

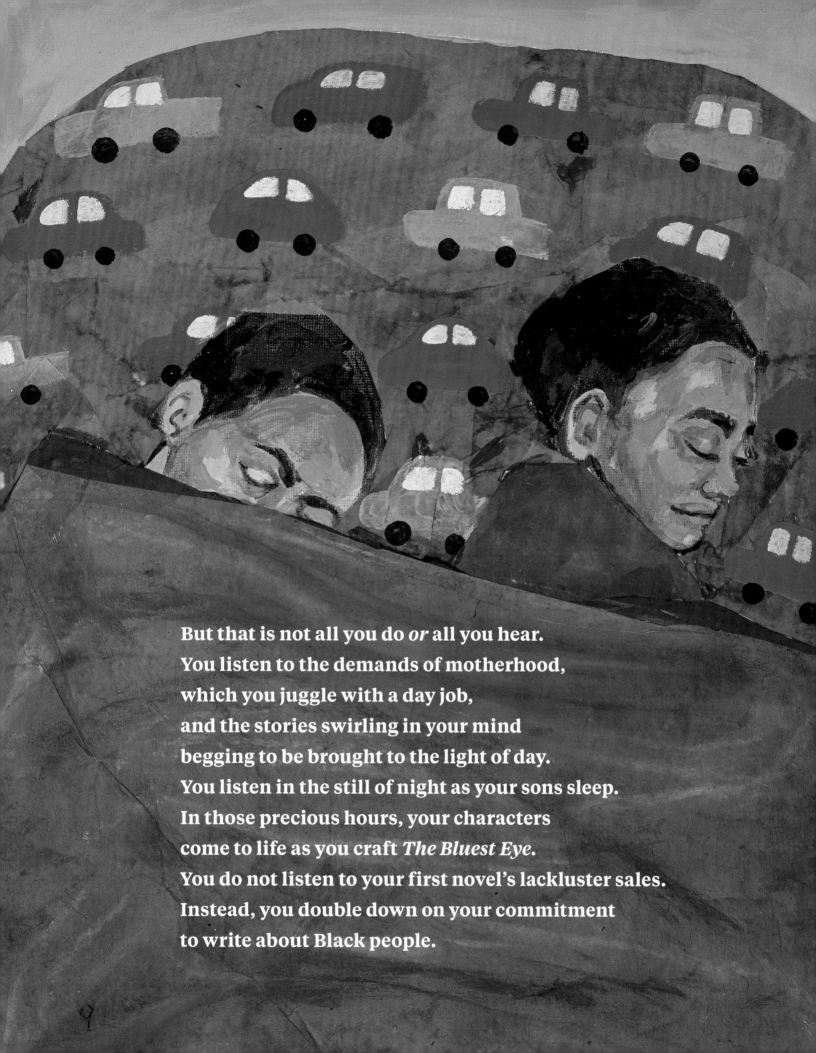

But that is not all you do *or* all you hear.
You listen to the demands of motherhood,
which you juggle with a day job,
and the stories swirling in your mind
begging to be brought to the light of day.
You listen in the still of night as your sons sleep.
In those precious hours, your characters
come to life as you craft *The Bluest Eye*.
You do not listen to your first novel's lackluster sales.
Instead, you double down on your commitment
to write about Black people.

You sift through
folklore, facts, and photographs
lovingly collected by amateur historians.
You compile five-hundred-plus images and artifacts
and moving quotes for
The Black Book—

a curious testament to the courage,
character, and contributions of brown folks
*who blazed trails and
beat odds.
Part scrapbook,
part time capsule.*

In its pages, you later find a news clipping
that inspires your masterpiece,

Beloved.

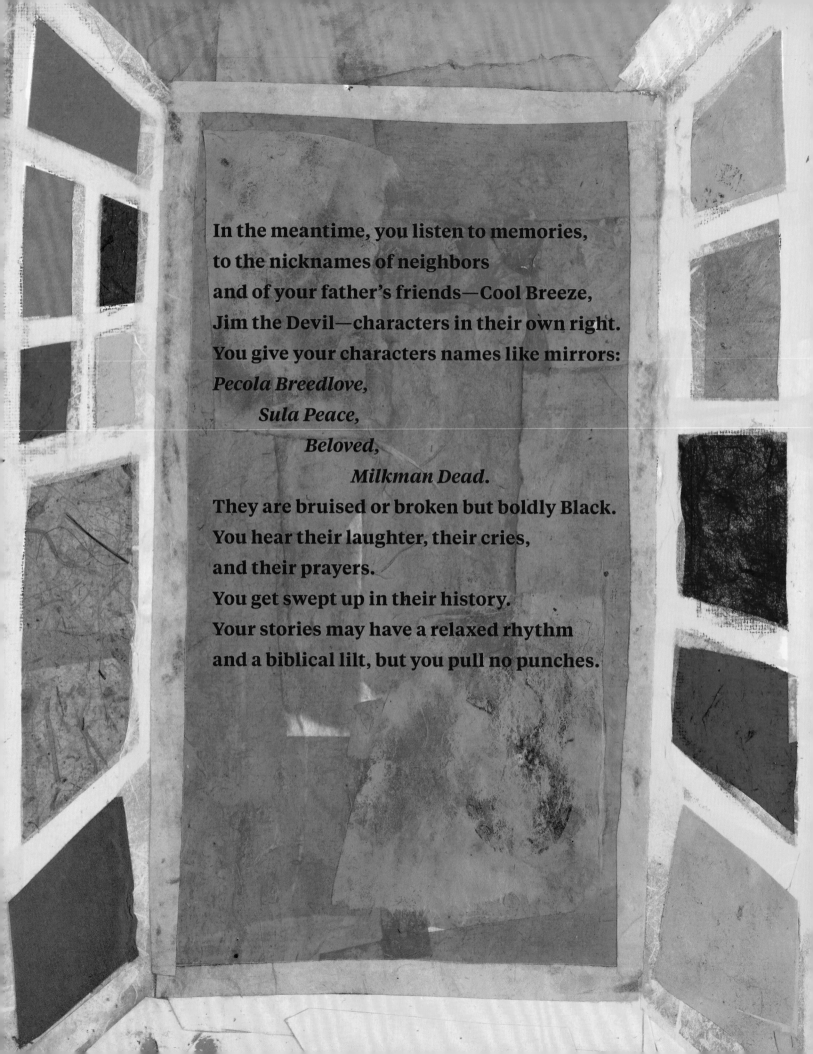

In the meantime, you listen to memories,
to the nicknames of neighbors
and of your father's friends—Cool Breeze,
Jim the Devil—characters in their own right.
You give your characters names like mirrors:
Pecola Breedlove,

    Sula Peace,

        Beloved,

           Milkman Dead.
They are bruised or broken but boldly Black.
You hear their laughter, their cries,
and their prayers.
You get swept up in their history.
Your stories may have a relaxed rhythm
and a biblical lilt, but you pull no punches.

You *never* shy away from hard truths.
You listen to the haunted and unholy places
that your characters call home:
your native Midwest; Lotus, Georgia;
Ruby and Haven, Oklahoma;
1920s Harlem; the Caribbean; and right here, right now.
They inhabit houses that are hurtful,
dreamlike, or deserted; rooms
with three doors and countless secrets.
You listen through the *window of Blackness*.
You echo the deep pain of our past
and *the vast possibilities of our future*.

What do you call your stories?
You title them
    Jazz,
        Beloved,
            Paradise,
                Home.

The sagas flow like rivers and span our history.
More than an author, you are a bridge.
If there is mercy, it is that for all our suffering
and striving, you chose to write about us.
You never listen to what other people say
about what you should create.
Instead, you listen to the silence for voices
that have been muted far too long.
You write the way you want readers to hear.
With your books in many languages,
readers hear you around the world.

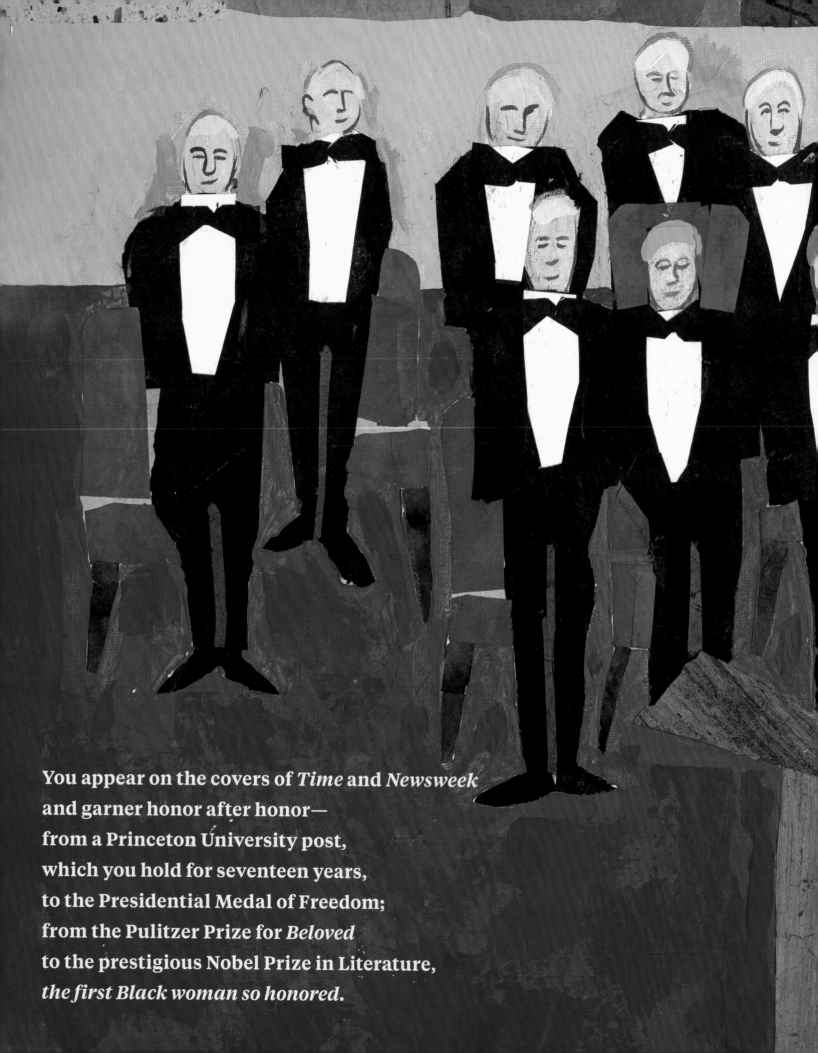

You appear on the covers of *Time* and *Newsweek*
and garner honor after honor—
from a Princeton University post,
which you hold for seventeen years,
to the Presidential Medal of Freedom;
from the Pulitzer Prize for *Beloved*
to the prestigious Nobel Prize in Literature,
the first Black woman so honored.

When you dine at the White House,
you listen as the first Black president, Barack Obama,
whispers in your ear. You are so giddy
that you completely forget what he said:
it was "*I love you*," and he spoke for us all.
You have given us stories that get under *our skin*,
next to *our hearts*, and inside *our souls*.

You listen to praise but do not rest on your laurels.
At your home beside the Hudson River,
with gray locs cascading down your back,
you plant tomatoes in pots
        and conjure stories
                beyond our imagination.

AUTHOR'S NOTE

In 1979, I took my first trip to California. At a bookstore in Berkeley, I bought *The Black Book*. A compilation of Black artifacts, primary source documents, and memorabilia, the book was a marvel to me. Never before had I seen such a wealth of Black culture in one place, let alone between the covers of a book.

As a graduate student in publications design in the 1980s, I was inspired by the design of *The Black Book* to pair my poems celebrating Black America with historic images. That photo-essay assignment for class grew into a lifelong passion for picture research. I would eventually visit archives such as the Library of Congress, the Schomburg Center for Research in Black Culture, and the Moorland-Spingarn Research Center at Howard University in search of historic images to accompany new and existing poems. Twenty years later, that class assignment grew into a book, *Remember the Bridge: Poems of a People*.

Over the years, I have returned to *The Black Book* again and again. I have read and studied many of Toni Morrison's novels, and I consider her a literary mentor. However, it was not until I wrote this biography that I realized she also conceived *The Black Book*. For that, I am eternally grateful.

TIMELINE

February 18, 1931: Toni Morrison, née Chloe Ardelia Wofford, is born in Lorain, Ohio, to Ramah and George Wofford.

1943: Chloe is baptized under the Catholic faith, and a priest chooses Anthony after Saint Anthony of Padua as her name, which leads to her nickname, Toni.

1953: Graduates from Howard University, earning a bachelor of arts in English

May 17, 1954: The US Supreme Court rules in *Brown v. Board of Education* that school segregation is unconstitutional.

1955: Earns her master of arts in American literature from Cornell University

December 5, 1955: The Montgomery Bus Boycott, protesting racial discrimination on public transit, begins in Alabama.

1957: Begins teaching English at Howard University

1958: Marries Harold Morrison, with whom she will have two sons, Ford and Slade

February 1, 1960: The Greensboro sit-ins begin with four Black students from North Carolina Agricultural and Technological College in nonviolent protest of segregated lunch counters.

1964: Marriage to Harold ends in divorce. The Civil Rights Act of 1964 prohibits discrimination in employment and in public spaces.

August 6, 1965: President Lyndon B. Johnson signs the Voting Rights Act.

1967: Begins working for Random House's trade book division in New York City and will eventually become the company's first female Black senior editor

April 4, 1968: Dr. Martin Luther King Jr. is assassinated in Memphis, Tennessee.

1970: *The Bluest Eye*, Morrison's first novel, is published.

1973: *Sula* is published.

1974: *The Black Book* is published.

1977: *Song of Solomon* is published.

1979: Awarded the Barnard Medal of Distinction, the college's highest honor

1981: *Tar Baby* is published.

1983: Leaves her job at Random House

1987: *Beloved*, her fifth novel, is published.

1988: Awarded the Pulitzer Prize for *Beloved*

1989: Receives an honorary doctorate of laws from Harvard University and joins the Princeton University faculty

1992: *Jazz* is published.

October 7, 1993: Becomes the first Black woman to win a Nobel Prize in Literature

December 25, 1993: An accidental fire burns Morrison's home in Rockland County, New York, destroying decades' worth of work, photographs, and family history.

November 6, 1996: Accepts the National Book Foundation Medal for Distinguished Contribution to American Letters

1998: *Paradise* is published.

1999: Morrison and her son Slade publish their first joint children's book, called *The Big Box*.

2005: Receives an honorary doctorate of letters from Oxford University

2006: After seventeen years at Princeton University, Morrison retires from teaching.

November 4, 2008: Barack Obama is elected as the first Black president of the United States.

November 11, 2008: *A Mercy* is published.

2010: Inducted as an officer of an elite French society called the Legion of Honor

2011: Receives honorary doctorates of letters from Rutgers University and the University of Geneva

2012: Awarded the Presidential Medal of Freedom by President Barack Obama

Home is published.

2015: *God Help the Child*, her eleventh novel, is published.

2017: Princeton University dedicates Morrison Hall in her honor.

The Origin of Others, a work of nonfiction, is published.

2018: Oprah Winfrey presents Toni Morrison with the Lifetime of Excellence in Fiction Award from the Center for Fiction.

August 5, 2019: Toni Morrison passes away at age eighty-eight in New York City.

BIBLIOGRAPHY

Als, Hilton. "Toni Morrison and the Ghosts in the House." *New Yorker*, October 19, 2003. www.newyorker.com/magazine/2003/10/27/ghosts-in-the-house.

Bollen, Christopher. "Toni Morrison's Haunting Resonance." *Interview*, May 1, 2012. www.interviewmagazine.com/culture/toni-morrison.

Ghansah, Rachel Kaadzi. "The Radical Vision of Toni Morrison." *New York Times Magazine*, April 8, 2015. www.nytimes.com/2015/04/12/magazine/the-radical-vision -of-toni-morrison.html.

Gross, Terry. "'I Regret Everything': Toni Morrison Looks Back on Her Personal Life." *Fresh Air*, NPR, August 24, 2015. www.npr.org/2015/08/24/434132724/i-regret-everything -toni-morrison-looks-back-on-her-personal-life.

Jaffrey, Zia. "The Salon Interview—Toni Morrison." *Salon*, February 2, 1998. www.salon .com/1998/02/02/cov_si_02int.

Kaiser, Mario, and Sarah Ladipo Manyika. "Toni Morrison in Conversation." *Granta*, June 29, 2017. www.granta.com/toni-morrison-conversation.

Morrison, Toni. "Toni Morrison—Nobel Lecture." NobelPrize.org, December 7, 1993. www.nobelprize.org/prizes/literature/1993/morrison/lecture.

Schappell, Elissa, and Claudia Brodsky Lacour. "Toni Morrison: The Art of Fiction No. 134." *Paris Review*, no. 128 (Fall 1993). www.theparisreview.org/interviews/1888 /toni-morrison-the-art-of-fiction-no-134-toni-morrison.

"Toni Morrison." Biography.com, May 6, 2021. www.biography.com/toni-morrison.

To Black writers of the past, present, and future.
—C.B.W.

I would like to dedicate these paintings to the life's work of Toni Morrison.
Her legacy and use of language will live on for many generations to come.

Thank you to my partner, Jairo Serna, whose love, patience, and support helped to
make this project possible. I couldn't have done it without you.

To Alison and Julia, who gave me the opportunity to work and collaborate on such a
book and held my hand every step of the way. I cherish you both.
—K.T.T.

PHOTO CREDITS

p. 3: Adapted from "Chloe Wofford as a young child," courtesy of the Special Collections of
the Lorain Public Library System.

p. 37: Adapted from a photo by Jack Mitchell/Archive Photos via Getty Images.

p. 39: Adapted from a photo by Roger Tillberg via Alamy.

p. 41: Adapted from a photo by Kevin Dietsch/UPI via Alamy.

Quill Tree Books is an imprint of HarperCollins Publishers.
A Crown of Stories: The Life and Language of Beloved Writer Toni Morrison. Text copyright © 2024 by
Carole Boston Weatherford. Illustrations copyright © 2024 by Khalif T. Thompson. All rights reserved.
Manufactured in Italy. No part of this book may be used or reproduced in any manner whatsoever without written
permission except in the case of brief quotations embodied in critical articles and reviews. For information
address HarperCollins Children's Books, a division of HarperCollins Publishers, 195 Broadway, New York, NY
10007. harpercollinschildrens.com. Library of Congress Control Number: 2022930097. ISBN 978-0-06-291103-2.
The artist used acrylic, oil paint, collage, handmade paper, and stencils on canvas board to create the paintings
for this book. Book design by Alison Donalty, Erin Fitzsimmons, and Julia Tyler.
24 25 26 27 28 RTLO 10 9 8 7 6 5 4 3 2 1
First Edition